# A BEAUTY OF A PLAN

by Angela Shelf Medearis

illustrated by Eric Velasquez

HOUGHTON MIFFLIN BOSTON • MORRIS PLAINS, NJ

California • Colorado • Georgia • Illinois • New Jersey • Texas

It was four o'clock on a sunny Wednesday afternoon. But there were still students hard at work at Meadow Middle School.

Mr. Flores ran the shop classes. Some days he let students stay late to work on their projects.

Sheila Ross and Michael DeWitt put the finishing touches on their cabinet.

"Wow!" Michael said. "This is our best work yet!"

Sheila and Michael cleaned up and got ready to go.

"Mr. Flores," said Sheila, "we're finished!"

Mr. Flores checked their work. "Looking good!" he said. "I can't wait to see the plans for your next project!"

"What about our next project?" Michael asked as he and Sheila walked home. "We need to hand in our plans by Friday."

Michael had designed the cabinet. Now it was Sheila's turn to plan a project. "Don't worry," she said. "I'll think of something. But right now I've got to run! You know my Grandma!"

Sheila rushed to her grandmother's beauty salon. Grandma depended on Sheila and her older sister Jackie to help out.

Sheila pushed open the door. The salon was full of chattering women and little girls.

Grandma kissed Sheila on her cheek. "Girl, where have you been?" she demanded.

"Grandma," Jackie said. "Sheila told us she would be late today. She had to finish a project for shop class."

Sheila gave her grandmother a hug. “Wait until you see the cabinet Michael and I made. Mr. Flores said it was really good! I love designing and building things.”

Grandma rolled her eyes. “Well, girl, I’d love it if you’d go upstairs and fold the towels.”

“Okay! Okay!” Sheila laughed.

Sheila went upstairs and got the towels. She sat down in the kitchen to fold them.

She smiled when she saw the snack on the table. Grandma had fixed her a sandwich and cut off the crusts from the bread. That was Grandma's way. She fussed at Sheila one minute and babied her the next.

After she finished with the towels, Sheila brought them downstairs. Then she started to sweep the floor.

Grandma came over and put her hand on Sheila's shoulder. "Why don't you drop shop class next semester?" Grandma asked. "Why waste time with hammers and saws?"

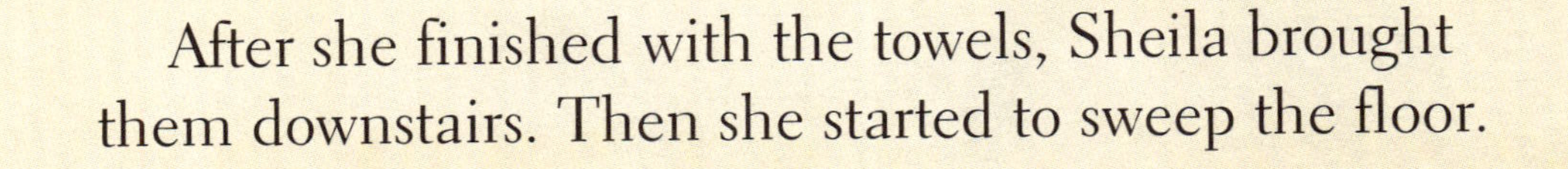

"When Jackie was your age," Grandma continued, "she was learning how to do hair. And now she's making money to pay for her classes in nursing school."

"Grandma!" Jackie said. "I enjoy doing hair. But that doesn't mean it's right for Sheila!"

Sheila shook her head. “I don’t want to do hair. I want to be an architect.”

“Face it, Sheila,” Grandma said. “This salon is how we earn our living. I’ll bet you can’t find a way to use what you learned in shop class here.”

Sheila looked around the salon. “I bet I can!”

"You're on!" Grandma said. "You have three weeks to prove that your shop class can help us here. If you do, I'll take over sweeping the salon for a month! But if you lose, you'll sweep—and you'll drop shop next semester."

"Fine," Sheila said calmly. "This will be easy!"

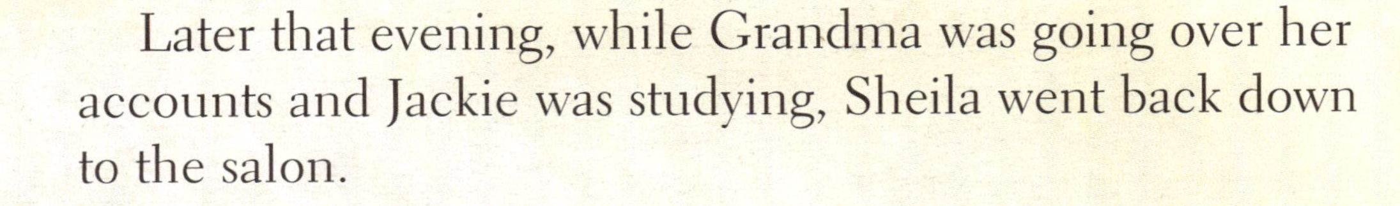

Later that evening, while Grandma was going over her accounts and Jackie was studying, Sheila went back down to the salon.

She took measurements and made sketches.

When she went back upstairs she was smiling.

The next day Sheila told Michael about the bet.

Michael looked worried. “So what’s your big plan?” he asked. “Do you need any help?”

Sheila laughed, “I can use all the help I can get! Jackie has already agreed to help, and so has my Uncle Al. He owns a carpentry business. Of course, I was hoping you’d help, too. I’m going to need a good cabinetmaker.”

Sheila showed Michael the sketches. "We'll build storage benches and cabinets for the beauty supplies," she said. "See—partitions, so everyone won't bump into each other. And here's a play area for little kids."

Michael's face relaxed. "Let's ask Mr. Flores if this can be our class project. Maybe some of the other kids in the class will help, too."

Before Sheila could say anything, Michael rushed over to talk to their teacher. Mr. Flores loved the idea. He called it "a great opportunity."

Mr. Flores had Sheila explain her plans to the class. Then he said that anyone who helped could get extra credit. Six other students signed up. Sheila and Michael got them started building cabinets.

A few days later, Uncle Al came to school. He brought large sheets of plywood, paint, and brushes.

"Thanks," Sheila told him. "Now we have everything we need."

The students finished building just before spring vacation began. By now the three weeks were almost up.

"The salon is closed on Mondays," Sheila said. "Grandma always leaves at eight o'clock to visit my aunt for the day. This Monday, Uncle Al will bring our stuff to the salon and help us install it."

At 8:30 on Monday morning Grandma was still reading the paper. Sheila didn't know what to say—everyone was coming at nine.

"Grandma," Jackie asked, "won't Aunt May worry if you're late?"

"I'm not going," Grandma said. "Since you're on vacation, we can spend the day together."

Sheila and Jackie looked at each other. If Grandma didn't go out, their plan would be ruined!

THE DAILY TIMES

Jackie sprang out of her chair. "Wonderful!" she said. "We can see the new exhibit at the museum. If we leave now, we can get there when the doors open."

Then Jackie turned to Sheila. "It's too bad you can't come with us," she said. "I know that you and Michael have to finish that project you've been working on."

"Yes, it's too bad," Sheila agreed.

She grinned as she watched them move briskly down the street. Jackie would keep Grandma busy all day.

Soon the sounds of hammers and drills filled the salon. “I feel like a real architect,” Sheila told Michael.

“Someday, you *will* be an architect,” Michael answered. Then he added shyly, “Maybe we can be partners then, too.”

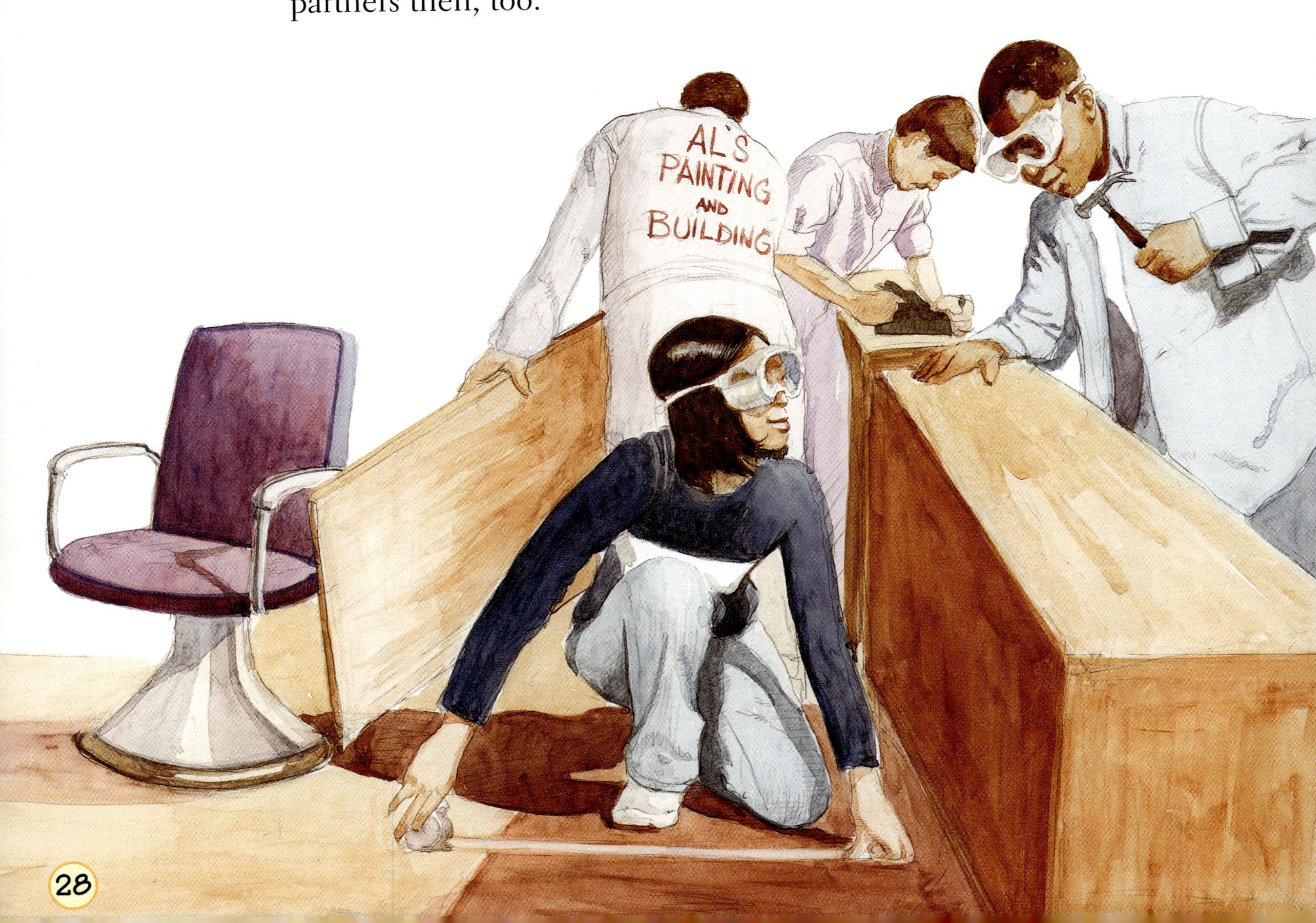

At six o'clock, Grandma and Jackie came back. "Surprise!" everyone shouted.

Grandma looked around the room. Then, without saying a word, she turned away and climbed the stairs.

Sheila's eyes filled with tears.

Jackie hugged her sister. She said, "Don't worry, I think Grandma just needs time to get used to the changes."

"I'll tell you what I think," said Grandma. She marched downstairs and towards Sheila.

There was a broom in her hand.

Grandma reached out to touch Sheila's cheek. "I think it's beautiful. Thank you! You've got a real talent for building things."

"Now move out of my way, girl!" Grandma said. "I've got some sweeping to do."